More Than Just a FLOWER GARDEN

Photos and Text by
Dwight Kuhn

Silver Press

To my mother and father

Acknowledgments: Thanks go to my wife Kathy for her
editorial help and her encouragement in the preparation of
this book. I also wish to thank Neil Soderstrom for his
valuable guidance and assistance from concept to final
books in this MORE THAN JUST A ... series. Thanks too to
this book's designer Andy Steigmeier and to Silver Press'
Bonnie Brook and Leslie Bauman, who helped in
shaping and designing the series.

Produced by Soderstrom Publishing Group Inc.
Book design by Andrew Steigmeier

Photos copyright © 1990 Dwight Kuhn
Text copyright © 1990 Dwight Kuhn and Soderstrom Publishing Group Inc.

Published by Silver Press, a division of
Silver Burdett Press, Inc.
Simon & Schuster, Inc.
Prentice Hall Bldg., Englewood Cliffs, NJ 07632

Library of Congress Cataloging-in-Publication Data

Kuhn, Dwight.
More than just a flower garden / text and photos by Dwight Kuhn. p.   cm.
Summary: Describes the living things in a flower garden, focusing
on the dynamic variety of plants and the creatures that depend on
them. Includes tips for starting yuor own flower garden.
1.Flowers—Juvenile literature. 2.Garden gardening—Juvenile
literature. 3.Garden ecology—Juvenile literature. (1.Flowers.
2.Flower gardening. 3.Garden ecology. 4.Ecology.) I.Title.
SB406.5.K84   1990   635.9—dc20   89-39511   CIP   AC
ISBN 0-671-69644-0   ISBN 0-671-69642-4 (lib. bdg.)

Printed in the United States of America

10 9 8 7 6 5 4 3 2 1

A flower garden is more than a colorful sight. It's a wonderful world of living things—an amazing, ever-changing world of plants and the creatures that depend on them. Yes, there is more to a flower garden than flowers. Much more.

People like to look at flowers. But hummingbirds and insects like to drink from them. Flying insects and hummingbirds spot colorful flowers from the air. Then they stop by to sip sweet-tasting nectar.

The hummingbird doesn't even land to take a drink. Its long bill and tongue reach deep inside each flower. Like a helicopter, a hummingbird can hover in one place. Its wings beat about 60 times a second, making a humming sound.

The butterfly keeps its tongue coiled under its head. After landing on a flower, the butterfly unwinds its tongue and drinks nectar.

Butterflies and other insects are cold-blooded. This means they must use the sun to help control their body heat. On warm sunny days, a butterfly flies a lot, seldom resting. Flying helps it cool its body. On cooler days, the butterfly rests on plants, spreading its wings to keep warm.

Petunias

Many flowers grow
only if you plant their
seeds in spring.
Others come up
year after year from
parts of plants
that wintered
underground.

Plants that live their
entire life in one
growing season are called
annuals. They sprout from
seeds, grow leaves, produce
flowers and seeds—and then
die. Some popular annuals
include petunias, marigolds,
sunflowers, geraniums,
zinnias, and snapdragons.

Plants that come up year
after year, without their seeds
sprouting, are called
perennials. Their underground
parts survive each winter
and sprout new plants each
spring. Lilies, tulips, daffodils,
irises, and lupines are all
perennials.

Tulips

Plants called *biennials* live their entire life in two years. "Bi" (pronounced *by*) means two. In its first year of growth, a biennial does not produce flowers.

Flowers form during the second year. Biennials die after their flowers have made seeds. Foxglove and sweet William are common biennials.

Sweet William

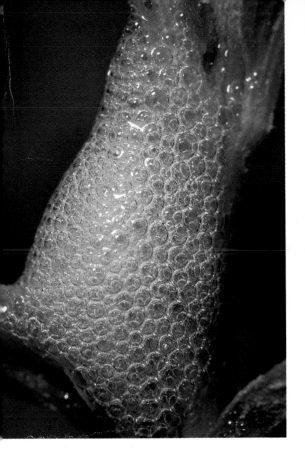

You may have noticed bubble masses on flower stems. If you gently clear away the bubbles, you will see a tiny spittlebug. The bubbles help keep the young spittlebug's skin from drying out. Protected by bubbles, the spittlebug grows wings and becomes an adult. Then it flies away. If you are gentle in clearing away the bubbles, you won't hurt the spittlebug. It will soon make more bubbles to repair its home.

9

Dwarf dahlia flower bud   **2nd day**

Most flowers develop from buds that form on stems. Green *sepals*, really tiny leaves, cover the colorful *petals* hidden inside. Once the sepals open, flower petals show. Soon the flower is completely open. Its colorful petals attract insects and hummingbirds to the nectar inside.

Flowers and their tasty green leaves also attract rabbits and hares. When rabbits and hares sense danger, they may simply freeze, hoping not to be seen. But often, they just dash to a safer place.

Snowshoe hare

The center of the lily flower has a female part called the *pistil*. This is a slender tube leading down to a swollen green *ovary* with eggs inside. Surrounding the pistil are male *stamens*. Tiny yellow grains of *pollen* form at the top of each stamen.

Tulip flowers have a pistil and stamens too. Can you find them?

When pollen from a stamen lands on a pistil, this is called *pollination* (pol-i-NAY-shun). Pollen then travels down the pistil's slender tube to the ovary, where it joins with an egg. This is called *fertilization* (fur-till-i-ZAY-shun). Now the egg becomes a seed. Often pollen from one flower travels to another flower. How does pollen get there?

Wind can carry pollen from the stamen of one flower to the pistil of another. Wind is an important pollinator for some flowers.

Insects are also important pollinators. Colorful flower petals and sweet nectar attract bees and other insects. As an insect crawls on the flower while sipping nectar, pollen sticks onto the insect. When the insect flies to another flower, some of this pollen may rub off onto the pistil of the new flower. Then the pollen travels inside the pistil to an egg and fertilizes it.

Honeybees carry a lot of pollen on their hind legs. What doesn't rub off on flowers is carried back to the beehive.

Both nectar and pollen are food for the bees. Bees store the nectar in the hive as honey. One bee needs to visit about 200,000 flowers to make a spoonful of honey.

Pollen on bee's hind leg

15

Stamens and pistil

These photos show how a daffodil develops seeds. Inside the flower are male stamens and a female pistil. Pollen-covered stamens surround the pistil.

After insects pollinate the flower, pollen reaches eggs in the ovary. The eggs become fertilized. Now they can become seeds.

As the ovary begins to swell, other flower parts die and fall away. Meanwhile, inside the ovary, many small white seeds are forming. Daffodil seeds turn black when they are fully ripe. Then the ovary opens and the seeds spill out.

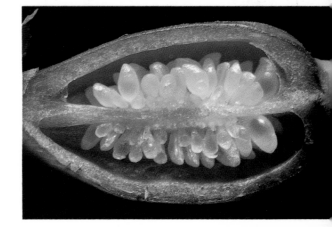

Ovary

Lupine flower

Lupines have many separate flowers on a single stem. As lupines make seeds, green seed pods replace the flowers.

Sunflowers produce seeds in the center of the flower. The yellow center will turn dark as the seeds ripen. Birds and other creatures love to eat sunflower seeds. While feeding on the seeds in the flower, birds knock some to the ground. And those seeds may sprout new sunflowers the following spring.

Rain and warmer temperatures make a sunflower seed swell. Soon it will grow roots down into the soil. Up from the ground comes a young sunflower seedling. The two seed leaves feed the baby plant. Later, other leaves will grow and make food for the plant.

Birds such as this goldfinch depend mainly on seeds for food. These birds may not make nests until midsummer. By then, many plants will have produced seeds. So that's the time the birds can find enough seeds to feed their hungry babies.

Goldfinch

Like all flowers, daffodils and irises can sprout from seeds. But, each spring, they can also grow from plant parts that wintered underground. Daffodils grow from an underground stem part called a *bulb.* Irises grow from rootlike stem parts called *rhizomes* (RYE-zomes).

Daffodil

Iris

Iris rhizome with stringlike roots

Roots take in water that contains soil *nutrients* (NEW-tree-ents) the plants need. Stems carry water and nutrients up into the leaves. Inside the leaves, green *chlorophyll* (KLOR-o-fill) helps the sun make food for the plant through *photosynthesis* (fow-tow-SIN-thes-sis). Here water from the soil and carbon dioxide from the air are changed into sugar and oxygen.

The plant uses the sugar as food. And it gives off oxygen to the air. All animals—including people—need oxygen from plants in order to breathe.

Many insects feed on plants. Aphids are harmful because they suck juices from stems and leaves. This may cause plants to die. You have to look closely to see one tiny aphid. These insects are smaller than the letters on this page.

In summer, only female aphids are born. Within one to two weeks, each baby grows up and has babies of its own. Before long, a plant is almost covered with the mother aphid and all her children and grandchildren.

Some garden insects are helpful. A large praying mantis eats grasshoppers and other insects. In the fall, the female mantis lays an egg case with several hundred eggs. Baby praying mantises are born the following spring. Each tiny mantis soon begins to gobble up aphids and other small insects.

Baby praying mantises

Crab spiders do not spin
webs like other spiders.
Instead they catch insects
by waiting on a flower, with
legs spread like a crab.
When an insect comes to a
flower for nectar, the spider
grabs it with its legs.

Some kinds of crab spiders can change part of their body color. On yellow flowers, they may turn yellow. On white flowers, they may turn white.

This camouflage helps the crab spider catch its next meal, such as this hoverfly.

Anole lizard

With tail growing back

Many kinds of animals find food in flower gardens. In the southern United States, the anole lizard hunts for insects and spiders in flower gardens. These lizards can quickly change color. They are brown when calm, but then turn bright green when excited.

Larger animals may try to catch an anole lizard. But if an animal grabs this lizard by the tail, it's in for a surprise. The tail stays behind. And the lizard runs to safety. Soon the lizard grows a new tail.

Many flowers have names that describe how they look. Learning the names of flowers can be fun. Can you guess which flowers match up with these names— black-eyed Susan, foxglove, and bleeding hearts? The answers are upside down near each photo.

Foxglove

Bleeding hearts

Black-eyed Susan

Flowers like these marigolds are beautiful. Yet the
flowers are just one stage— an important stage— of a
plant's growth. From flowers come seeds. And from
seeds, new plants can grow. As we've seen, flower
gardens also help many kinds of creatures.

Yes, there's more in a flower garden than you might
imagine. Much more.

Starting Your Own Flower Garden

Starting Plants Indoors: Some plants need more time than others to grow and flower. You can give them a head start by planting them indoors in early spring. Then when the weather and soil are warmer, you can transplant them outdoors in a flower box or garden.

1 These are some of the things you will need. Buy clean potting soil mix from a garden store. Don't use garden soil because it may have diseases, insects, or weed seeds. You could also buy plant containers called trays or peat pots. Milk cartons or drinking cups work well too.

2 Use a nail to punch holes in the bottoms of drinking cups or milk cartons. This lets water drain out. Peat pots don't need holes because water can drain through them. Some trays have ridges along the bottom for water to drain into, so holes are not necessary. Fill the containers with the special potting soil mix.

3 Write the name of each plant on a small stake or Popsicle stick, using a pencil or waterproof ink. Push in the stake along the edge of the container. Then place two seeds in each container. That way, if one seed doesn't sprout, the other probably will. In trays, place seeds 3 inches (8cm) apart. Sprinkle the seeds with just enough soil to cover them. Then pat the soil softly with your fingers.

4 Gently water. If the water uncovers the seeds, push the seeds back into the soil. Water only until the soil looks evenly moist.

5 Keep the seeds and containers indoors in a warm place. A tray underneath will catch any water that leaks through. When the soil begins to dry out, moisten with a mister or small sprinkling can. Use just enough water to keep the soil moist. If the soil gets too dry, young plants may die.

6 When plants begin to sprout, put the containers in a warm sunny spot indoors. Water them, but don't overwater. The soil should be moist, not soaking wet. If more than one seed sprouts in a container, use scissors near the soil to cut off all but the healthiest sprout. This is called thinning. In a tray, thin seedlings if they grow closer than 3 inches to one another.

Getting the Flower Box Ready: When your seedlings are about 4 inches (10cm) tall, they are almost ready to be transplanted outdoors. But first they need to get used to being outdoors. So place the plants in their container outdoors for about a week in a partly shady place.

7 Your window box should have holes in the bottom. And it should be raised above the surface it rests on. This lets water drain out. Cover the bottom with gravel or stones. Then add soil.

8 The plants will need food to help them grow. You can buy plant food at a garden store. Or you can use homemade plant food called *compost*, made from decayed plants and leaves. Mix the soil well with whatever plant food you choose.
To learn how to make compost, see page 39 under "compost."

9 Before transplanting, water the seedlings in their containers. In your flower box, make a hole in the soil. Make the hole bigger than the clump of soil and roots you will put in the box. Then, while holding each plant upside down, carefully shake it from its container. If you are taking plants from a tray, dig out each plant's roots and soil with a trowel or a large spoon. Be careful not to cut off many root ends. Place the root clump into the hole.

10 Cover the roots with soil, and then water thoroughly.

Planting Seeds Directly into the Garden: Many flowers do not need to be started indoors. You can plant their seeds directly into the garden. But first, turn the soil over with a shovel. Remove other plants already growing there. Try to make the soil loose and crumbly.
Rake it smooth and level.

1 Place a stake to mark the end of the seed row. Then stick the seed package on top. Starting at the stake, use a stick to make a straight furrow. Directions on your seed package will tell you how deep and how far apart the seeds should be. Place the seeds in the furrow.

2 Cover the seeds with dirt. Then water the whole row.

Planting Flower Bulbs: Some flowers are started from bulbs or other underground parts instead of seeds. These bulbs sprout new plants each year. Dig a hole where you want each bulb. To help the plants grow, add compost and bone meal. Place the bulb, pointed end up. How deep should you plant the bulb? Follow the directions that come with it. Cover with soil.

Gladiola bulb

Bearded irises and day lilies

Glossary and Index

annual (ANN-you-all), page 6
Any plant that lives for only one growing
season. "Annual" means one.

biennial (by-EN-ee-all), page 8
Any plant that produces flowers and seeds in its
second year of growth and then dies. "Bi" means two.

bulb (BULB), page 22
A roundish underground stem part.
Bulbs grow flowers year after year.

Bulb

chlorophyll (KLOR-o-fill), page 23
Green coloring in plants. Leaf chlorophyll
changes water and air into plant food.

compost (KAHM-post), page 35
A soil-like mixture of decayed plants and leaves.
Compost is rich in nutrients that plants feed on. To
make compost for the next year, place leaves and old
garden plants into a pile. Add dirt or manure. Mix a
few times in the summer.

fertilization (fur-till-i-ZAY-shun), page 13
When pollen joins with an egg to form a seed.

nutrients (NEW-tree-ents), page 23
The important ingredients in food that help plants
and animals grow and stay healthy.

(Continued)

ovary (OH-va-ree), page 12
The swollen part of the pistil. The ovary contains eggs.

perennial (per-EN-ee-all), page 6
Any flower plant that sprouts up from underground parts
year after year. A perennial can also grow from a seed.

petals (PET-uls), page 10
Usually the biggest flower part—and usually not green.
Petals attract bees and other insects.

photosynthesis (fow-tow-SIN-thes-sis), page 23
The making of food within plant leaves. Photosynthesis
changes water and air into food when light shines on leaves.

pistil (PIS-tul), page 12
The female part of a flower.

FLOWER PARTS

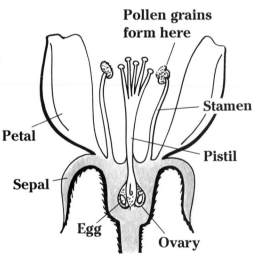

pollen (POL-in), page 12
Dustlike grains on the tip of a stamen.

pollination (pol-i-NAY-shun), page 13
When pollen lands on a pistil.

sepals (SEE-pulls), page 10
The leaflike parts that protect a
flower bud. Usually sepals are green.

stamens (STAY-mens), page 12
Male parts of flowers that make dustlike
grains called pollen.